Dentists

by Kristin L. Nelson

↳ Lerner Publications Company • Minneapolis

Lerner Publications Company
A division of Lerner Publishing Group
241 First Avenue North
Minneapolis, MN 55401 USA

Website address: www.lernerbooks.com

Words in **bold type** are explained in a glossary on page 31.

Library of Congress Cataloging-in-Publication Data

Nelson, Kristin L.
    Dentists / by Kristin L. Nelson.
      p.   cm. – (Pull ahead books)
    Includes index.
    ISBN: 0–8225–1688–8 (lib. bdg. : alk. paper)
    1. Dentists–Juvenile literature. I. Title. II. Series.
RK63.N445 2005
617.6–dc22   2004019584

Manufactured in the United States of America
1 2 3 4 5 6 – JR – 10 09 08 07 06 05

What kind of doctor looks in mouths
and says "open wide"?

3

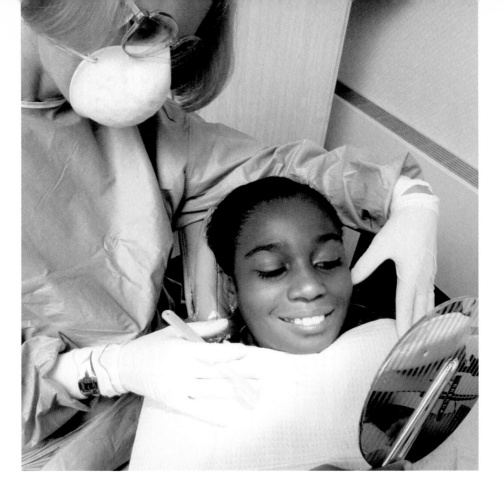

A dentist! Dentists make sure teeth
and mouths stay healthy.

Dentists work in offices in your
community. Your community is made
up of people in your neighborhood,
town, or city.

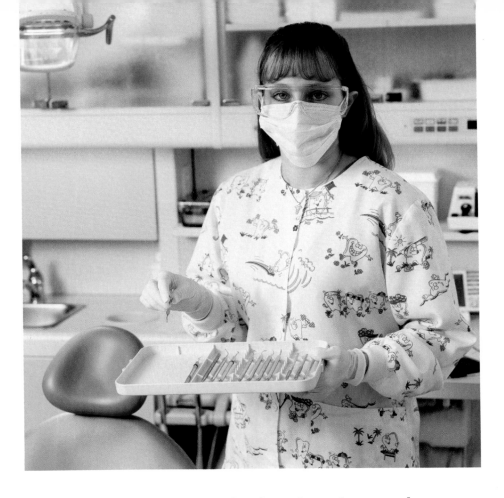

Hygienists often help dentists. A hygienist is someone who cleans teeth.

People who visit dentists are called **patients.** Have you visited a dentist?

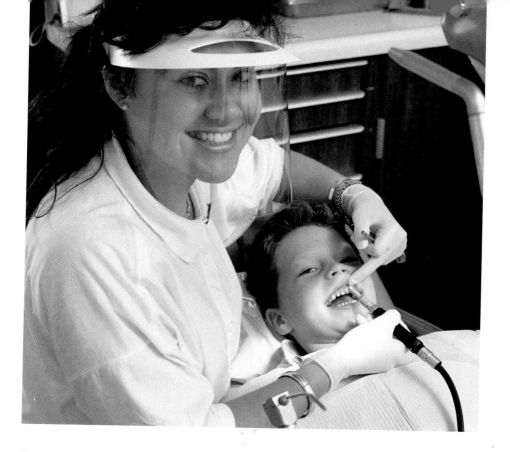

Most patients go to the dentist twice a
year for **checkups.** What happens at
a checkup?

Dentists look closely at teeth. They wear masks and gloves to keep **germs** from spreading between patients.

Patients sit in a special chair. The chair moves up and down. It tips back and forth too.

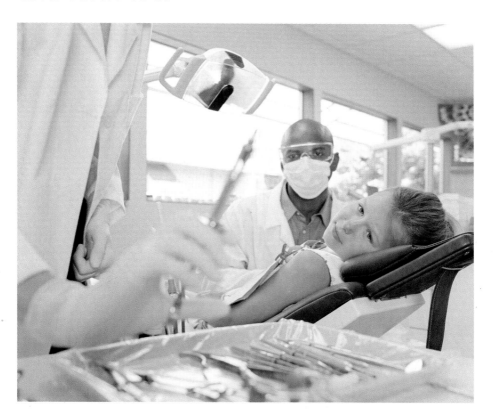

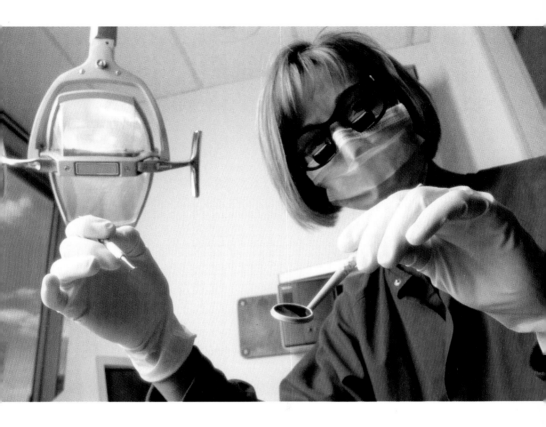

A bright light and a little round mirror
help dentists see. What are dentists
looking for?

They look for **plaque.** Plaque is a thin, sticky layer caused by tiny pieces of food. It builds up when teeth aren't brushed daily.

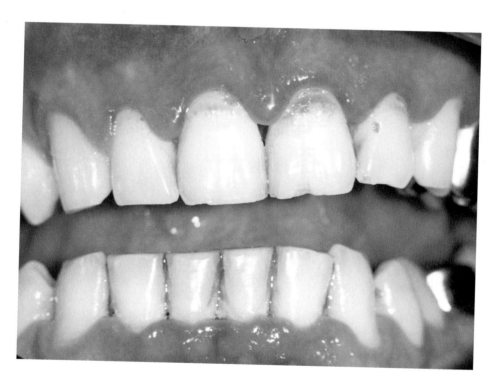

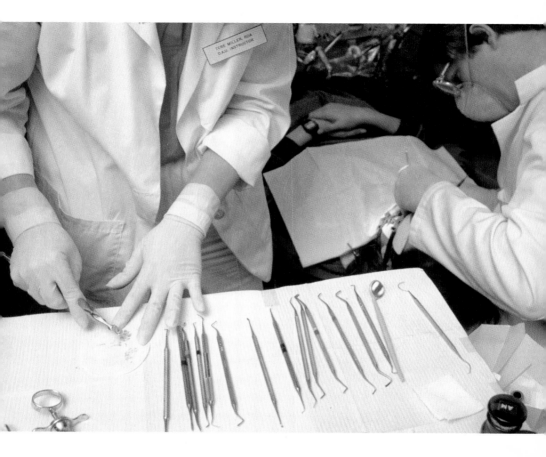

Dentists remove plaque before it harms teeth. They use tools to scrape it away.

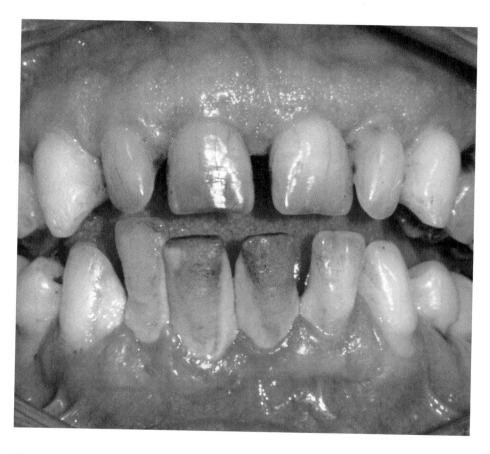

These teeth need a dentist! Too much plaque makes teeth soft and rotten.

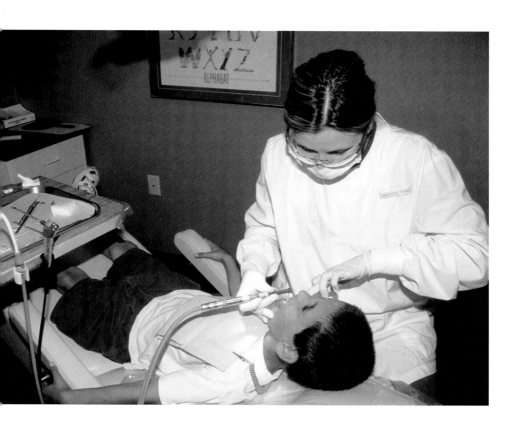

Whirr! Dentists clean and polish teeth
after plaque is gone. They use a tool
with a spinning rubber tip.

It's time to floss between the teeth.
Flossing removes stuck food.

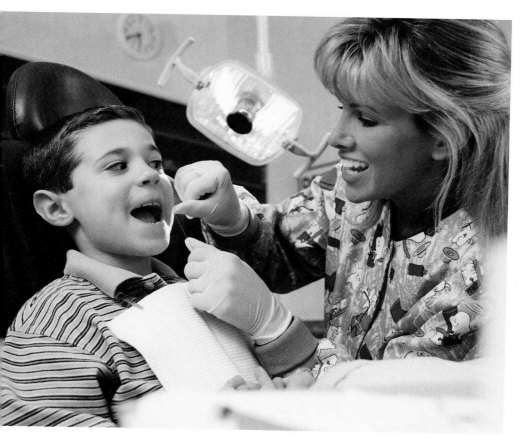

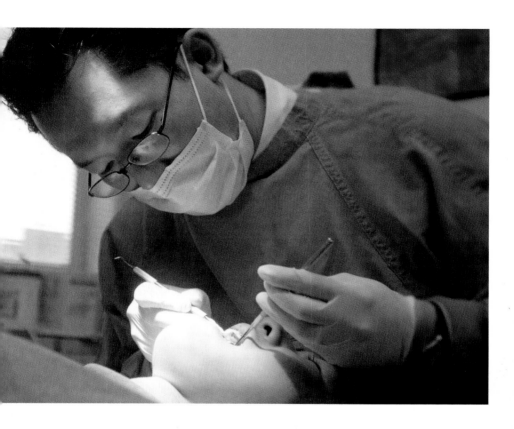

Next dentists check for **cavities.**
A cavity is a small soft spot in the
tooth. How do dentists find them?

Dentists use a tool called an **explorer.**
It can reach into small places.

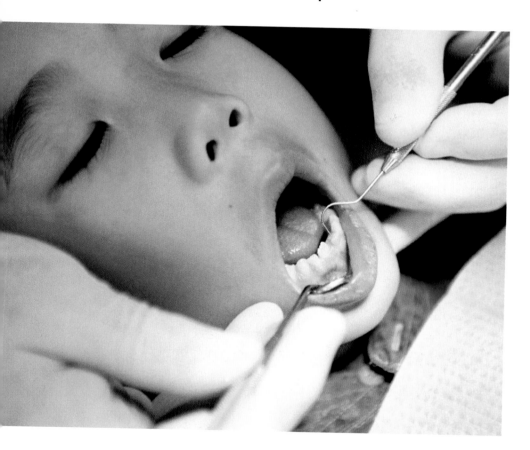

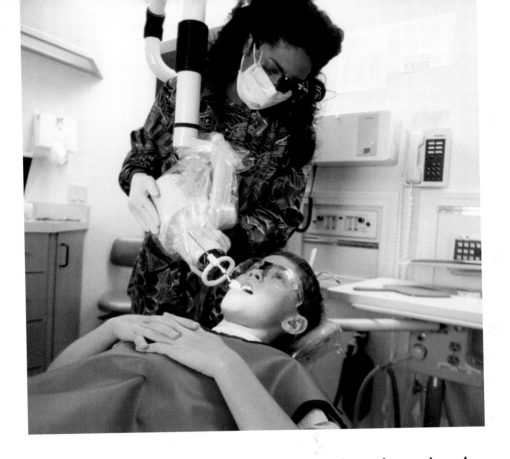

An **X-ray machine** helps dentists look for cavities too. What does this machine do?

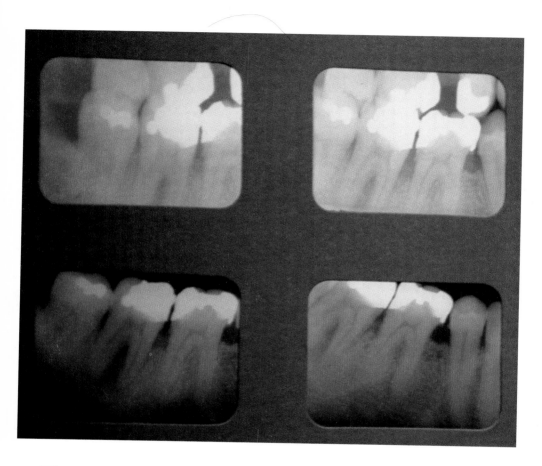

The machine takes pictures. The pictures show hard and soft parts of teeth.

Dentists take out the soft part with a drill. They fill the hole with a hard material called a **filling.**

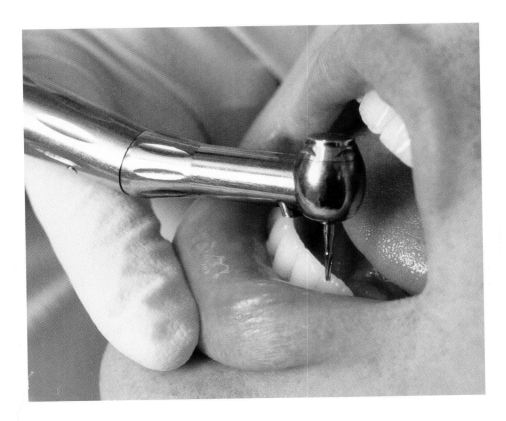

Then dentists teach patients about good **hygiene.** Hygiene is how you keep your body clean and healthy.

Flossing and brushing daily are good hygiene. Good hygiene and regular checkups stop problems such as cavities.

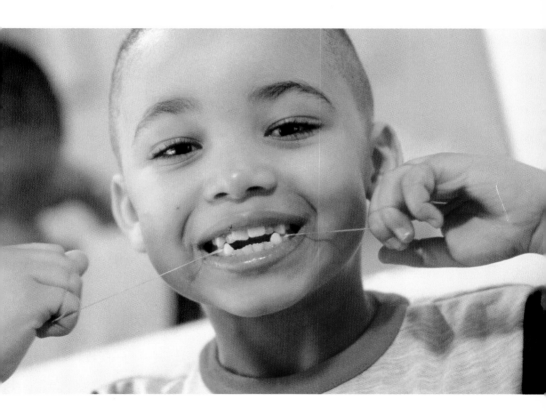

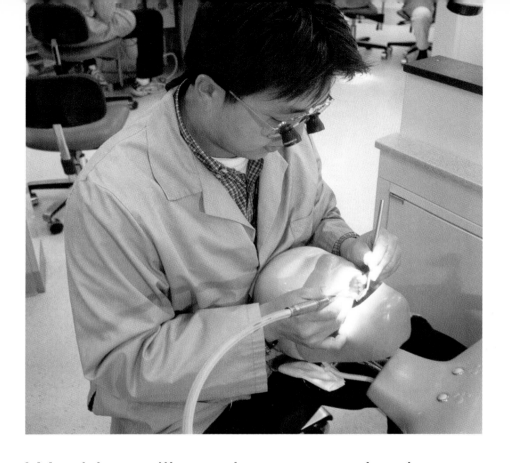

Would you like to become a dentist someday? People study for many years to work as dentists.

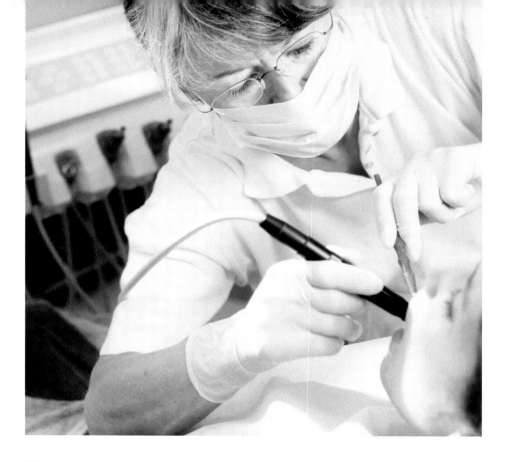

Dentists need good eyesight to work with teeth. They have to be good with their hands too.

Dentists have an important job. Dentists help keep teeth clean and healthy.

Having healthy teeth is something you can really smile about!

Facts about Dentists

■ Some dentists put braces on teeth. Braces help crooked teeth become straight. These dentists are called orthodontists.

■ A person must go to college for eight years to become a dentist.

■ Dentists work with more than just teeth. They fix problems with the bone and skin around teeth too.

■ The pink skin around teeth is called gums.

■ Some dentists are surgeons! They do operations on teeth and gums when needed. They are called oral surgeons.

■ If a tooth is causing a patient a lot of problems, a dentist may have to pull the tooth.

Dentists through History

- In the late 1800s, an American dentist used his mother's spinning wheel to turn a drill.

- In the late 1800s, an Englishman invented a toothbrush made with cow's hair!

- George Washington had false teeth. They were made from elephant ivory tusk and hippopotamus tusk. False teeth are also called dentures.

- Before toothbrushes were around, people used to chew on sticks after meals. The sticks scraped the plaque from people's teeth.

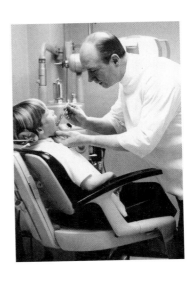

- In the 1800s, a dentist told people to use silk thread as dental floss.

More about Dentists

Check out these books and websites to find out more about dentists.

Books

Murkoff, Heidi. *What to Expect When You Go to the Dentist.* New York: HarperFestival, 2002.

Berenstain, Stan, and Jan Berenstain. *The Berenstain Bears Visit the Dentist.* New York: Random House Books for Young Readers, 1981.

Keller, Laurie. *Open Wide: Tooth School Inside.* New York: Henry Holt & Company, 2000.

Gorman, Jacqueline Laks. *Dentist.* Milwaukee: Gareth Stevens Publishing, 2002

Websites

KidsHealth
http://www.kidshealth.org

The American Dental Association
http://www.ada.org

Glossary

cavities: soft places or holes in teeth caused by plaque

checkups: regular visits to the dentist for cleaning and care of teeth

community: a group of people who live in the same area

explorer: a special tool used to find cavities

filling: a material used to fill in a cavity

germs: tiny living things that can make people sick

hygiene: cleanliness for good health

hygienists: workers who clean teeth and help dentists

patients: people who visit the dentist

plaque: a thin, sticky layer that can be found on teeth

X-ray machine: a device that takes detailed pictures

Index

Photo Acknowledgments

The photographs in this book appear courtesy of: © Royalty-Free/CORBIS, front cover, pp. 6, 9, 10, 16, 21, 26; © Richard Heinzen/SuperStock, p. 3; © Bluestone Productions/SuperStock, p.4; © BananaStock/SuperStock, p. 5; © Tom Stewart/CORBIS, pp. 7, 19; © SuperStock, Inc./SuperStock, pp. 8, 29; © PhotoDisc/Royalty-Free by Getty Images, pp. 11, 18, 20; © CNRI/Photo Researchers, Inc., p. 12; © Phil Schermeister/CORBIS, p. 13; © SPL/Photo Researchers, Inc., p. 14; © Jack Ballard/Visuals Unlimited, p. 15; © Roger Allyn Lee/SuperStock, p. 17; © Jim Cummins/CORBIS, p. 22; © Jon Feingersh/CORBIS, p. 23; © Jim Sugar/CORBIS, p. 24; © Image Source/SuperStock, p. 25; Brand X Pictures, p. 27.